MADE IN PARACORD!

25 great jewellery, accessories and home projects to knot

CAITLIN WYNNE

Search Press

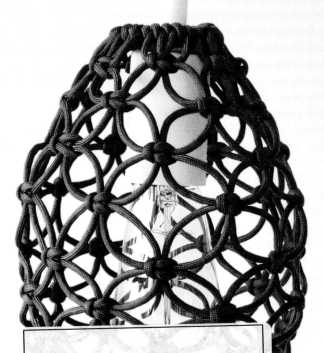

CONTENTS

WELCOME TO CAITLIN'S WORLD

'I like minimalism. I like to be different. But most of all, I love innovation.

During my studies at Denmark's Design School in Copenhagen, I discovered the art of macramé. I'd never considered myself a 'crafter' or even an artist; I was a designer. But what I realised as I quickly became fascinated with macramé was that this textile art had it all, and I wanted to be its creator.

I was first drawn to the craft after stumbling across a vintage shop in Copenhagen devoted to macramé plant hangers from the 1970s. I'd never heard of macramé before, but my love of nature drew me to these amazing works of art. I immediately had to learn. I started creating beach terrariums to sit inside the plant hangers. For me, this was perfection. After years of collecting shells from beaches across the world, I had an opportunity to give them a purpose. I found great joy in crafting the terrariums and giving people the possibility to grow something natural in their homes that required minimal upkeep. As people became increasingly charmed by my macramé hangers with beach terrariums, I became more immersed and started to build a reputation as a crafter of macramé.

Less is more.

Macramé is straightforward and rope is all you need to create a world full of simple, innovative and beautiful things. I explored the craft using all kinds of rope, and paracord became a favourite of mine because of its large range of colours and its incredible weatherproof durability. I believe in creating pieces that will last a lifetime, pieces that can be passed on from generation to generation and live to tell the story.

I'm inspired by Scandinavian design and driven by my affection for nature. These particular passions have come together in a unique style, which is driven by the use of my hands as my tools. There is so much freedom in using your hands to craft and create - the world of exploration is more intimate and exciting

For this book, I have chosen projects both big and small - projects to give you a base of skills to start your journey into macramé and others to give you ideas of what's possible. I want this book to be the inspiration for creating pieces that are not only beautiful but also innovative. For this is why I love macramé: it is not just about creating pieces of beauty, but also about creating things the world needs.

And, in return, making our world a more beautiful place.

PARACORD AND THE ART OF MACRAMÉ

Macramé using paracord is a rewarding craft that offers endless creative opportunities. Before you start your projects, learn a little more about paracord and where to find this versatile material. Find out about what tools you will need and where to buy them. Then let's look at the importance of colour when working with paracord, and explore some palettes that will kick-start your own design ideas.

Paracord

Paracord, also known as parachute cord, was originally used for the suspension lines of parachutes during World War II. It soon became a widely used multi-purpose cord due to its exceptional strength, lightness and weatherproof nylon outer shell. These qualities make it a perfect craft cord.

There are a few different types and thicknesses of paracord, but the one most commonly used and readily available is the 550 cord. As its name suggests, this type of cord has a breaking strength of 550lb, which is 250kg.

Paracord 550 is easy to find and relatively inexpensive. The most convenient place to buy it is online, where you will be able to choose from a large range of colours and lengths. Paracord colours can vary greatly among suppliers, with some colours sharing the same name but being completely different shades. Therefore, if you require specific colours, it's safest to look around your local hardware shops or to ask the online shop for colour samples before purchasing.

YOU AND YOUR TOOLS

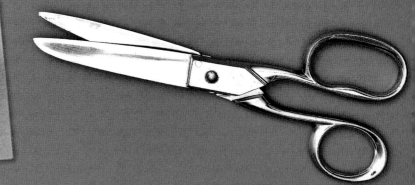

There is a list of specific tools to accompany each project in this book, but you will need these three basic tools for all projects:

· Scissors
· Lighter
· Measuring tape

Additionally, you will find it useful to buy an S-hook, which you can hang over a door handle, curtain rod or similar fixture. You can then attach the project piece to the hook to give a firm and comfortable base on which to work. This set-up can be worked both vertically and horizontally, depending on whether you sit or stand to macramé. If you're sitting, you might find that the S-hook is too high for easy knotting. This is fixed by tying some rope to the hook to adjust the height.

EXTRA BITS AND PIECES

Some of the projects in this book solely use paracord, while others require additional materials, such as buckles and jewellery clasps. To find these materials, first try your local hardware or craft shop. If you have no luck there, turn to the web. Websites such as eBay and Etsy are great places to buy jewellery findings, beads, thread, secondhand objects and even paracord.

CAUTION

Please take care when working on your paracord projects, particularly when you are melting, gluing and slicing.

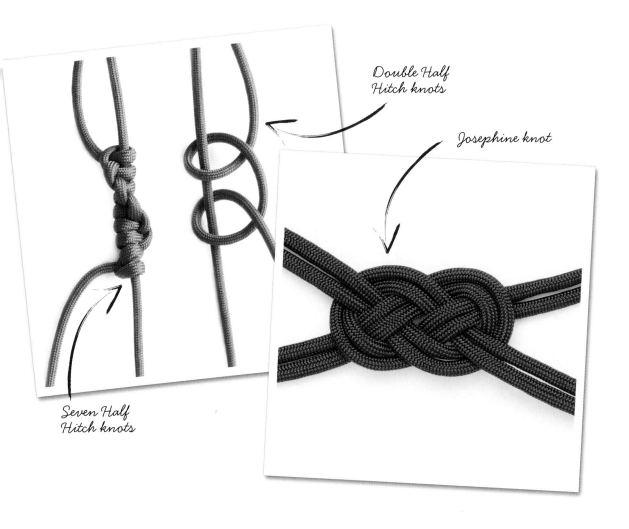

Double Half
Hitch knots

Josephine knot

Seven Half
Hitch knots

KNOW YOUR KNOTS

On pages 114-127 of this book, you will find step-by-step instructions for all the macramé knots used in these projects, from the Turk's Head to the Alternating Square. First of all, familiarise yourself with all the knots – and practise them till they start to come naturally! Once you have mastered the knots, you'll have the knowledge to set your creativity free and craft amazing objects. Each project in this book has been designed to get you started, but also to leave room for your innovations. Use these projects as guides and a jumping-off point for your own creativity.

CRAFT YOUR COLOUR

Colour is central to any craft design. When planning each paracord project, take time to consider which of the hundreds of colours, tones, patterns and finishes will best create the look you are going for. If you are feeling overwhelmed with choices, take a look at the examples of different colour palettes in this book. You may find them useful when exploring with colour to find your own style.

COLOUR AND KNOT
When designing your pieces, one question to ask yourself is if the colour of your paracord complements the knot you're using. Knots can be simple or very complex, which may affect your choice of paracord. For example, multicoloured, patterned paracord might not suit a very complex knot.

EARTHY TONES OR NEON BRIGHTS
When you're selecting colours, be sure they belong to the same 'colour expression'. Pick one colour expression and run with it – but don't mix them up, as they don't work together. If you're going with bright colours, then own them and go crazy. If you're choosing subtle or earthy tones, control them and make your piece beautiful.

Complex knots look best in plain colours

Earthy tones

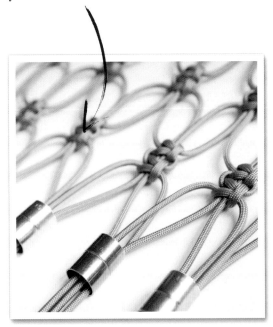

GLOSSY OR MATTE

Paracord can be purchased in either a glossy or a matte finish. The cord is not often advertised as 'gloss' because traditionally it's always made of glossy nylon. However, some suppliers offer paracord with more of a matte finish. Explore both options.

Keep in mind that it's often best to remain with one finish for a project. The two finishes can complement each other perfectly, but only on occasion. For example, using two matte colours and a glossy metallic within the same colour expression can look great.

SCRAP AND SPRAY

As you knot your way through the pages of this book, you're likely to develop a large scrap cord pile of random colours. To recycle your scraps, purchase a can of spray paint and spray them! Alternatively, craft a project out of scrap colours and then spray it when it's finished.

Matte cord

JEWELLERY PROJECTS

SIMPLE BANGLE

*This minimalist bangle uses the traditional Turk's Head knot.
Despite being both beautiful and strikingly modern, it is a simple
enough piece to get you started with paracord and macramé.*

DIMENSIONS
◯ 23cm (9in) maximum
inside circumference

MATERIALS & TOOLS
4m (13ft) of paracord
1 glass, can or similar
    round object
Measuring tape
Scissors
Sellotape
Lighter

INSTRUCTIONS

1 Measure and cut a length of paracord:
1 × 4m (13ft).

2 Tape one end of the cord to your round object. The
round object is going to help you keep the desired
bangle size and shape as you start to work.

3 Working around your round object, complete three
rotations of the Turk's Head knot (see page 121). Ensure
that the second and third rotations are parallel to the first.
The cord should start and end on the inside of the bangle.

4 When you have completed three rotations, cut off the
excess cord, leaving 5mm (¼in) at both ends. Using the
lighter, melt both ends and press them down together with
your scissors. Ensure they are melted flat and are hidden on
the inside of your bangle.

NOTE
Use a round object – such as a
glass or can – of the right
circumference to create a bangle that
will fit your wrist comfortably.
Try experimenting with a piece of
string (or your own favourite bangle)
to find the right circumference.

KNOTS NEEDED FOR PROJECT

Turk's Head knot (see page 121)

SIMPLE NECKLACE

If you're looking for an easy project that's also creative and stylish, this one is for you. This necklace involves only one basic knot, but lets you explore your creativity with different tones, colours and patterns.

DIMENSIONS

↔ Four balls, each 2.5cm (1in) in diameter

MATERIALS & TOOLS

4m (12ft) of paracord in various colours
1 chain or leather necklace
Measuring tape
Scissors
Lighter
1 large blunt needle

INSTRUCTIONS

1 Measure and cut your lengths of paracord: 4 × 1m (3ft).
Be creative with your choice of colours.

2 Using your four different-coloured lengths of paracord, complete four Monkey Fist knots (see page 124).

3 To cleanly finish each ball, cut off any excess paracord from the ends. Using the lighter, melt each of the ends and press them inside the ball using your scissors. Remember that the ends must be hot and melting when pressed into the balls, to ensure that your knots don't unravel.

4 Using the large blunt needle, thread your chain or leather necklace through the middle of each ball. Make sure you thread the needle through the same spot on each ball to create an even necklace.

NOTE
You can be creative with the number of Monkey Fist knots you create. A variety of different looks can be achieved by including more or fewer.

KNOTS NEEDED FOR PROJECT

Monkey Fist knot (see page 124)

KNOTS NEEDED FOR PROJECT

Chain Sinnet knot (see page 124)

STATEMENT NECKLACE

Make a statement with this bold macramé necklace, in which the chunky texture of a Chain Sinnet knot is contrasted with delicate embroidery thread. Whether you treat yourself or make it for a friend, everyone will want to know where you bought it.

DIMENSIONS

↕ 38cm (15in) maximum

MATERIALS & TOOLS

8m (26ft) of paracord
3 colours of embroidery
   thread
2 end caps with 1cm (³/₈in)
   diameter
1 jewellery joining (1 lobster
   clasp and 2 rings)
Measuring tape
Scissors
Superglue
Pliers

INSTRUCTIONS

1 Measure and cut your paracord into these lengths:
   4 × 2m (6¹/₂ft).

2 Gather all four of your lengths of paracord together –
   you will be working with them as if they were one thick
cord. Measure 30cm (12in) down from one end of the
paracords. This is where you will begin the Chain Sinnet knot
(see page 124).

Four paracords used as one thick cord

Start your Chain Sinnet knot 30cm (12in) from one end (Step 2)

3 Work your Chain Sinnet knot until you have completed seven loops.

When you have made seven loops, your chain is complete

4 Using your first colour of embroidery thread, wrap it round the cords at one end of the Chain Sinnet chain. Create an even coil that extends around 5cm (2in) along the paracords. Wrap tightly over the starting end of your thread to secure it. When you have made your coil, tie together your two loose ends, then cut them to about 1.5cm ($^5/_8$in).

First colour of embroidery thread extends for 5cm (2in) along the paracord

Loose end secured under second colour of thread (Step 5)

Even coils of thread

5   Choose your second colour of embroidery thread. Start to coil it round the paracords, overlapping with your first colour of thread to hide its loose ends. Continue for 5cm (2in) along the paracords. Tie together and cut off the loose ends, as in Step 4.

6   Repeat Step 5 with your third colour of embroidery thread. Tie the ends of your thread and tuck inside the coil to hide them.

7   Repeat Steps 4-6 at the other end of the Chain Sinnet knot.

8   Cut both ends of your paracord to your desired necklace length. Glue each of the paracord ends, then press them into the end caps. When the glue is dry, attach the jewellery joinings using pliers.

NOTE
Be creative with your choice of colours for your paracord and embroidery threads. A variety of looks can be achieved by working with subtle texture and tone changes or by going bright and contrasting.

SURVIVAL BRACELET

This bracelet makes the perfect 'man bangle'. He might be amused to know that, as the name implies, this bracelet could literally save his life. Made from one long piece of paracord, it could be unraveled in moments in an emergency!

DIMENSIONS

↕ 25cm (10in) maximum

MATERIALS & TOOLS

3m (10ft) of paracord
1 U-type buckle
Measuring tape
Scissors
Lighter

INSTRUCTIONS

1 Measure and cut a length of paracord:
1 × 3m (10ft).

2 Using your measuring tape, measure the required wrist size then add 4cm (1½in) for the correct bracelet length. You will need to know this measurement for Step 4.

3 Undo the U-type buckle so that you have two parts. Using the end of your length of paracord, make a Lark's Head knot (see page 115) in the middle of the U part of the buckle.

4 Using your measurement from Step 2, measure the correct bracelet length down the cord from the buckle. Then double back the paracord, making a loop and returning to the U part of the buckle.

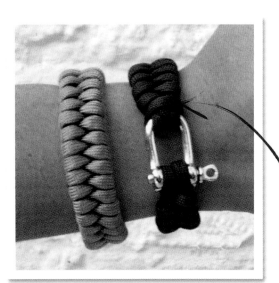

Lark's Head knot

KNOTS NEEDED FOR PROJECT

Lark's Head knot (see page 115)
Fishtail knot (see page 125)

5 Thread the working end of the paracord behind the U and through the front of the Lark's Head knot.

Working end of paracord is threaded behind the U and through the front of the Lark's Head knot (Step 5)

U part of buckle

Loop is the correct bracelet length

To start the Fishtail knot, take the working end behind first (Step 6)

Working cord

6 Now you can begin the Fishtail knot (see page 125). Start the knot by going behind first.

7 Continue your Fishtail knot down the paracord until you have a 4-cm (1½-in) loop at the end. Leave the working end of the paracord so that it is lying loose over the top of the bracelet.

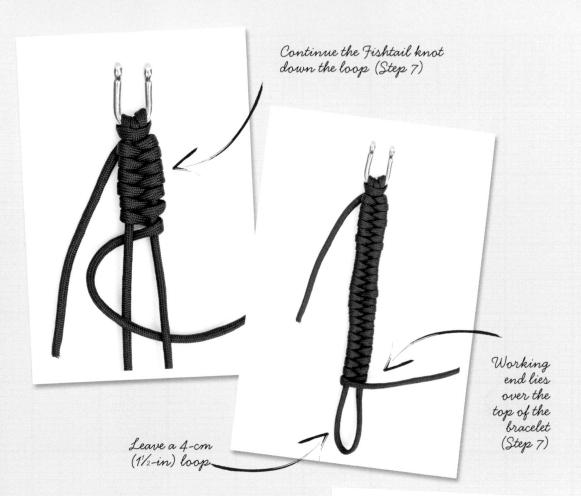

Continue the Fishtail knot down the loop (Step 7)

Working end lies over the top of the bracelet (Step 7)

Leave a 4-cm (1½-in) loop

8 Wrap the working end of the paracord over the loop to split it into two smaller loops.

9 Cut both ends of the paracord down to 8mm (⅓in). Using the lighter, melt the ends. Stick them to the inside of the bracelet by pressing with scissors. To attach the bracelet, put the two small loops between the holes in the U part of the buckle and screw the buckle peg through the buckle holes and the loops.

BRACELET WITH BLING

In this quick project, you will be working with an essential macramé knot, the Square knot. By adding a piece of copper tubing to your design, you'll create a gorgeous piece of handmade jewellery with a touch of modern bling.

DIMENSIONS
↕ 25cm (10in) maximum

MATERIALS & TOOLS
2.6m (8½ft) of paracord
1 piece of copper tubing: the
   bracelet shown opposite
   uses a tube 1.5cm (⅝in)
   in diameter and 2.5cm
   (1in) long
Measuring tape
Scissors
Lighter

NOTE
These lengths of paracord will make a bracelet 25cm (10in) long. You may need to shorten the cords to fit your wrist comfortably.

INSTRUCTIONS

1 Measure and cut your paracord into lengths of the following sizes:
    1 × 60cm (2ft)
    1 × 2m (6½ft)

2 Take the 60cm (2ft) length of paracord. Double it over and knot together the ends with an Overhand knot (see page 115). This looped cord will form the backbone of your bracelet. The length of cord you need will depend on your wrist size. Remember that the bracelet will shrink as you work, so make sure you will be able to fit two fingers between the bracelet and your wrist.

Form a loop in the 60-cm (2-ft) paracord (Step 2)

Overhand knot at bottom of the loop

KNOTS NEEDED FOR PROJECT

Overhand knot (see page 115)
Square knot (see page 116)

Looped cord

Tie a Square knot around
the looped cord (Step 3)

3 Now take the 2-m (6½-ft) length of
paracord. Working from the middle of
this cord, you are going to make continuous
Square knots (see page 116) around and
down the looped cord until you reach the
knot at the bottom. Tie your first Square
knot 1.5cm (⅝in) below the top of the
looped cord. This will leave a loop large
enough to fit the knot at the bottom of the
cord – this is how you will wrap the bracelet
around your wrist.

2-m (6½-ft) length
of paracord

Leave a loop
1.5cm (⅝in)
long (Step 3)

Make continuous Square knots
down the looped cord

4 When you have continued your Square
knots all the way down to the knot at
the bottom, cleanly cut off all excess cord.
Using the lighter, melt the ends onto the
inside of the bracelet.

5 Thread the bracelet through the copper
tubing until it reaches the middle. The
Overhand knot that you made in Step 2 can
be pushed through the loop you made in
Step 3 to fasten and unfasten the bracelet.

JOSEPHINE BRACELET

The Josephine knot is traditionally known as a Sailor's knot because it is commonly used for joining two ropes. Luckily for us, it's very simple to produce and can be used to create a stunning bracelet design.

DIMENSIONS
↕ 25cm (10in) maximum

MATERIALS & TOOLS
3m (10ft) of paracord in the colour or colours of your choice
2 end caps with 1cm (³⁄₈in) diameter
1 jewellery joining (1 lobster clasp and 2 rings)
Measuring tape
Scissors
Superglue
Pliers

INSTRUCTIONS

1 Measure and cut these lengths of paracord: 6 × 50cm (20in).

2 Take two of your lengths of paracord. Working in the middle of both cords, tie them into a Josephine knot (see page 120). Take another two lengths of paracord and repeat the knot again, tracing your steps from the first knot so that these cords lie next to the original cords. Repeat for a third time with your final two cords. Ensure that the second and third knots are parallel to the first, with no twists.

3 Measure the bracelet around your wrist, then cut the ends to the desired length.

4 Glue an end cap onto each end of your paracord. Using pliers, fix on the jewellery joining.

NOTE
Be creative with colours and tones. Just a slight change in colour can completely change the look of this bracelet.

KNOTS NEEDED FOR PROJECT

Josephine knot (see page 120)

ACCESSORIES PROJECTS

LANYARD

Lanyards are usually really dull – designed to do nothing more than dangle a key or whistle. This project gives the uninteresting lanyard a new lease of life. With symmetrical knotting, it is so beautiful that it could be a necklace.

DIMENSIONS

↕ 60cm (24in) maximum

MATERIALS & TOOLS

5m (16½ft) of paracord
2 colours of embroidery
    thread
1 split ring
2 end caps with joinery ring
Measuring tape
Scissors
Masking tape
Superglue

KNOTS NEEDED FOR PROJECT

Half Hitch knot (see page 118)
Double Half Hitch knot (see page 118)

INSTRUCTIONS

1 Measure and cut these lengths of paracord:
2 × 2.5m (8¼ft).

2 Thread one length of paracord through the split ring until the ring is in the middle. If you want to hold it steady, you could stick the split ring to your work surface with masking tape.

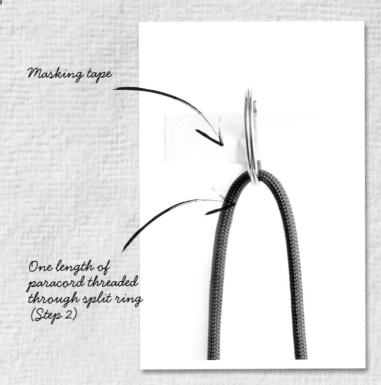

Masking tape

One length of paracord threaded through split ring (Step 2)

NOTE
Remember that your lanyard
needs to be symmetrical. Try to
make your knots mirror those
on the opposite side.

3 Take your second length of paracord. Fold it in half and place it under the first cord. This second length will be your working cord for now.

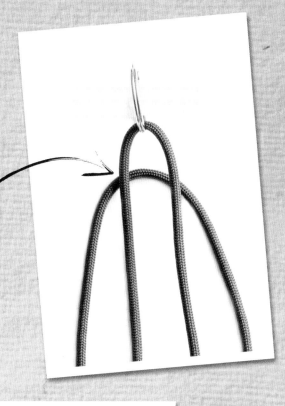

Second cord folded in half and placed under first cord (Step 3)

4 With your working cord, make a Double Half Hitch knot (see page 118) over the left-hand length of the first cord. Repeat for the right-hand length.

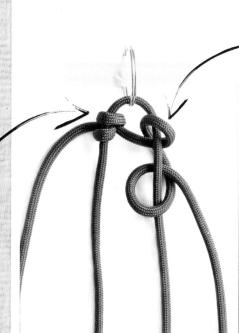

Double Half Hitch knot on right-hand side (Step 4)

Double Half Hitch knot on left-hand side (Step 4)

Double Half Hitch knots
[these are the top two]

Eight Half
Hitch knots
(Step 5)

5 Now make eight Half Hitch knots (see page 118) on the left-hand cord. Then make eight Half Hitch knots on the right-hand cord. You're creating a symmetrical design, so make sure that the two sides mirror one another.

6 On each side, swap the working cord to the other length. Leaving a 6-cm (2½-in) gap, make a Double Half Hitch knot over the old working cord on the left-hand side. Repeat on the right-hand side.

6-cm
(2½-in)
gap

Double Half
Hitch knot
(Step 6)

7 Complete seven Half Hitch knots on both sides.

8 Using your first colour of embroidery thread, wrap it around the two inside cords in the 6-cm (2½-in) gap. Make an even coil about 1.5cm (⅝in) long. Wind your coil around the starting end of your thread in order to secure it. When you have made your coil, tie together your two loose ends. Tuck them inside the coil to hide them.

Double Half Hitch knots [the ones at the top]

Seven Half Hitch knots (Step 7)

Coil of embroidery thread in colour one (Step 8)

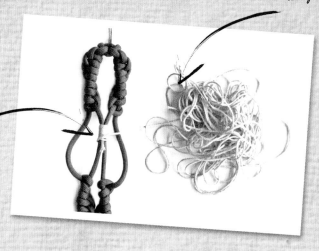

Loose ends tied together to secure

10-cm (4-in) gap

Coil of embroidery thread in colour two (Step 9)

9 Take your second colour of embroidery thread. Wrap it around the cords on each side of the lanyard, 10cm (4in) above the knot chain. Secure the thread in the same way as in Step 8.

10 Now return to your first colour of embroidery thread. Wrap it directly above the coil you have just added. Secure the thread as described in Step 8.

11 At your desired lanyard length, cut the cords. Glue the end caps onto the ends. Attach the joinery ring.

SIMPLE LANYARD

This variation on the lanyard project features a minimalistic design and can be completed in less than 30 minutes. Simple and understated, it is the perfect gift for a gentleman.

Make a 4-looped Slide Knot around a split ring

Cleanly cut then melt both ends to finish

Make a 4-looped Slide Knot (see page 119) around a clasp

1.5m (5ft) of paracord will make a lanyard 1m (3ft) long

KEY CHAIN

Upgrade any set of keys with a handmade Globe knot key chain. This is the perfect project if you are interested in learning a complex knot.

DIMENSIONS
↕ 8cm (3in)

MATERIALS & TOOLS
1m (3ft) of paracord
1 split ring
1 wooden ball or bead of
    15mm ($^5/_8$in) diameter
Measuring tape
Scissors
Lighter

INSTRUCTIONS

1 Measure and cut a length of paracord:
1 × 1m (3ft).

2 Complete a Globe knot (see page 123) around your wooden ball or bead.

3 With the working cord, push a 5-cm (2-in) loop out of the top of the knot.

4 To finish, cleanly cut your ends and then melt them together using the lighter. Hide your melted ends inside the knot. Attach the split ring to the loop.

SHOPPING BAG

There's no need for plastic shopping bags when you can craft your own environmentally friendly one. This design requires four different knots, so it is a great project for those wanting to develop their macramé skills further.

DIMENSIONS
↕ 1m (40in) maximum

MATERIALS & TOOLS
18m (60ft) of paracord
4 jewellery end caps of 1cm
  (³/₈in) diameter
Measuring tape
Scissors
Superglue

INSTRUCTIONS

1 Measure and cut your paracord into these lengths:
   6 × 3m (10ft).

2 Group your six lengths of paracord into three pairs. In the middle of all three clusters, make a Crown knot (see page 122).

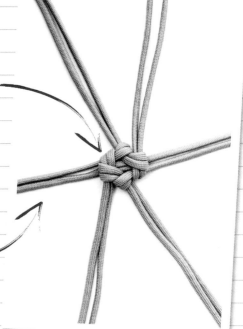

Crown knot in middle
of lengths (Step 2)

Six lengths of paracord,
grouped into pairs

KNOTS NEEDED FOR PROJECT

Crown knot (see page 122)
Alternating Square knot (see page 116)
Square knot (see page 116)
Three-Strand Braid knot (see page 126)

Leave 3cm (1¼in) between rows

First row of Alternating Square knots (Step 3)

Second row of Alternating Square knots

3 You now have 12 working lengths. Working outwards from your Crown knot, complete seven rows of Alternating Square knots (see page 116). Leave 3cm (1¼in) between each row.

NOTE
When tying your Alternating Square knots in Step 3, lay the piece flat on a table for ease of working.

Square knot (Step 4)

Three-Strand braid knot (Step 5)

4 Now divide the lengths into two groups of six cords. These groups will become your two bag straps. Lay the bag flat on a table for ease of working. Working with one of your two groups, make a Square knot (see page 116) with the outer four lengths over the inner two lengths.

5 Complete a Three-Strand Braid knot (see page 126) until you reach your desired strap length.

6 To complete the other strap, repeat Steps 4 and 5 using your second group of lengths.

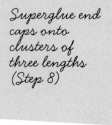

Superglue end caps onto clusters of three lengths (Step 8)

Join the two straps using a Square knot (Step 7)

7 Using a Square knot, join the two straps together.

8 Evenly cut the excess cord to your desired tassel length. Using superglue, stick the four jewellery end caps onto the ends (working with four clusters of three).

KNOTS NEEDED FOR PROJECT

Carrick Bend knot (see page 120)

HEADBAND

This headband design can be adapted to suit all ages.
With only one knot and minimal paracord required,
it makes for the perfect quick project.

DIMENSIONS
⭕ 45–65cm (18–25in)

MATERIALS & TOOLS
2.5m (8ft) of paracord
6cm (2½in) of 12mm (½in)
    wide elastic (woven
    elastic is best)
1 elastic hair band
Measuring tape
Scissors
Lighter
Superglue

INSTRUCTIONS

1 Measure and cut your paracord into lengths of the
following sizes:
1 × 1m (3ft)
1 × 1.5m (5ft)

2 Using the 1-m (3-ft) length of paracord, complete a
Carrick Bend knot (see page 120). Make as many repeats
of the knot as you desire. Finish by melting the paracord
ends together and hiding them under the knot.

Melted and flattened ends on underside of knot (Step 2)

Carrick Bend knot using 1-m (3-ft) length of paracord

3 Measure both your head circumference and the length of the hair band (when slightly stretched). Subtract the length of the hair band from your head circumference. Using your 1.5m (5ft) of paracord, cut three pieces of paracord to this measurement. Cleanly melt all the ends of the paracord so that they don't fray.

4 Thread the three lengths of paracord through the underside of the Carrick Bend knot.

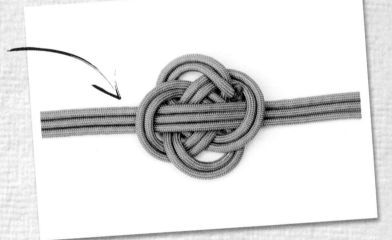

Three lengths of paracord threaded through underside of knot (Step 4)

Three lengths of paracord superglued to elastic (Step 5)

5 Now cut your woven elastic into two 3-cm (1¼-in) lengths. Superglue one end of the headband approximately a third of the way up one length of elastic.

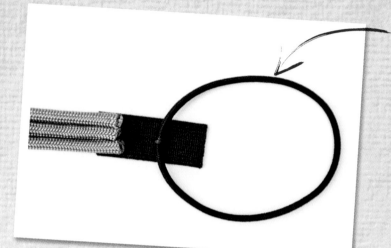

Hair band placed on elastic, ready for gluing (Step 6)

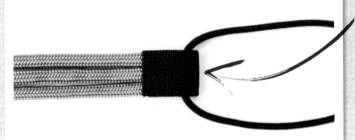

Elastic glued onto cord ends, creating a loop (Step 6)

6 Loop the elastic through the hair band, then glue the elastic down on top of the cord ends.

7 Repeat Step 6 for the other end of the headband, so that both sides are attached to the hair band.

BELT

Do you have an old, unused belt lying around? Strip out all its fabulous assets to create a whole new addition to your wardrobe. This quick and easy project offers plenty of room for creativity.

DIMENSIONS
↕ 1m (3ft) maximum

MATERIALS & TOOLS
10m (32ft) of paracord
1 belt buckle around 3.2cm
    (1¼in) wide
1 belt tip around 2.5cm (1in)
    wide
Measuring tape
Scissors
Lighter
Superglue (optional)

INSTRUCTIONS

1 Measure and cut your paracord into these lengths:
4 × 2.5m (8ft).

2 Working in the middle of each length of paracord, complete a Lark's Head knot (see page 115) over the belt buckle. Attach all four lengths of paracord in this way.

3 Now make a Four-Strand Braid knot (see page 126), using each doubled length of paracord as one strand.

4 Once you have reached your desired length, cut and melt the paracord ends. Many belt tips come with a screw to attach them. Using this, or superglue, attach your belt tip securely.

5 If you'd like to add a belt loop, make use of a scrap piece of paracord. Loop it around the belt and melt the ends together.

NOTE
If you don't have an old belt that you can strip for its hardware, belt buckles, tips and screws are easy to find online, both from specialist suppliers and from general hardware or craft shops.

KNOTS NEEDED
FOR PROJECT

Lark's Head knot
(see page 115)
Four-Strand Braid knot
(see page 126)

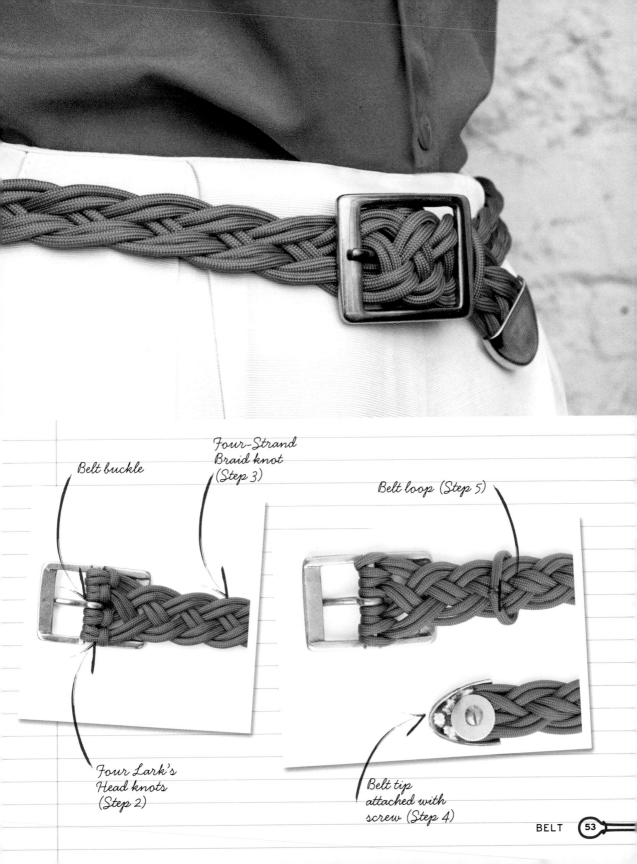

Belt buckle

Four-Strand
Braid knot
(Step 3)

Belt loop (Step 5)

Four Lark's
Head knots
(Step 2)

Belt tip
attached with
screw (Step 4)

KNOTS NEEDED FOR PROJECT

Lark's Head knot (see page 115)
Six-Strand Braid knot (see page 127)

WATCH STRAP

There is nothing better than recycling old pieces from your drawer – or vintage treasures picked up in a secondhand shop. This fun project is simple in design but gives you the chance to modernise an overlooked watch.

DIMENSIONS
↕ 25cm (10in) maximum

MATERIALS & TOOLS
3m (9ft) of paracord
1 watch face and buckle
Measuring tape
Scissors
Lighter

INSTRUCTIONS

1 Measure and cut your paracord into these lengths: 3 × 1m (3ft).

2 Measure the circumference of your wrist, then add 5cm (2in) to this measurement. This will be the length of your watch strap.

3 Gut each length of paracord by pulling out the strands of white cord inside.

4 Working at the middle of each length of paracord, complete a Lark's Head knot (see page 115) over the watch buckle. Attach all three of your lengths of paracord in this way.

Watch buckle

Lark's Head knots (Step 4)

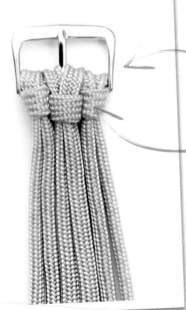

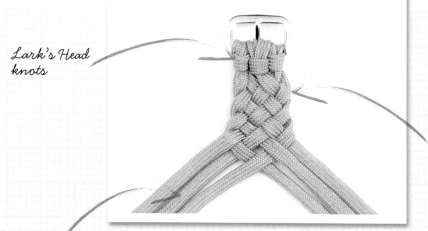

Lark's Head knots

Six-Strand Braid knot (Step 5)

Flatten cord with your fingertips as you work

5 Now make a Six-Strand Braid knot (see page 127).

6 Once you have reached your desired length (as measured in Step 2), slide the watch face onto the strap.

NOTE
As you make your Six-Strand Braid knot, flatten the paracord with your fingers. This will give the strap a smoother and more comfortable finish.

7 To finish, weave the cord ends through the underside of the strap. You only need to weave each length once. Then cut your ends, melt them and press down onto the underside of the strap using scissors. Make sure the ends are melted flat so that you can pass the strap through the watch buckle.

8 To add a strap loop, use a scrap piece of paracord. Loop it around the strap and melt the ends together.

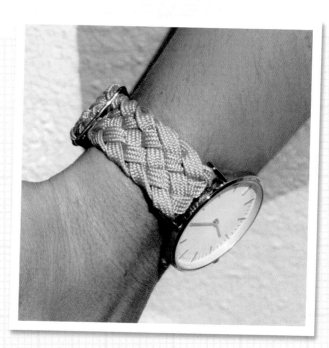

Optional strap loop

Cord ends cut, melted and pressed flat

Weave cord ends into the underside of the strap

CAMERA STRAP

When you're travelling, you probably carry your camera everywhere. Standard camera straps are very workaday – so make sure yours is a fashion statement by crafting one for yourself.

DIMENSIONS
⬍ 1m (3ft) maximum

MATERIALS & TOOLS
24m (80ft) of paracord
1 long pearl head pin
1 piece of leather at least
    10 × 12cm (4 × 5in)
2 small split rings
Measuring tape
Scissors
Sewing machine or
    superglue

INSTRUCTIONS

1 Measure and cut your paracord into these lengths:
8 × 3m (10ft).

2 For ease of working, line up all your eight lengths on a flat surface. Thread the pearl head pin through the top of them all. Now we will assign letters to our eight lengths, working from the left: D, C, B, A, A, B, C, D. This means that the two middle cords are both A, while the two outer cords are both D, and so on.

Cords are assigned letters for ease of working (Step 2)

Pearl head pin

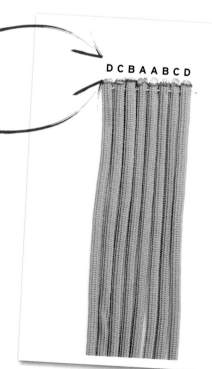

D C B A A B C D

KNOTS NEEDED FOR PROJECT

Square knot (see page 116)
Half Hitch knot (see page 118)

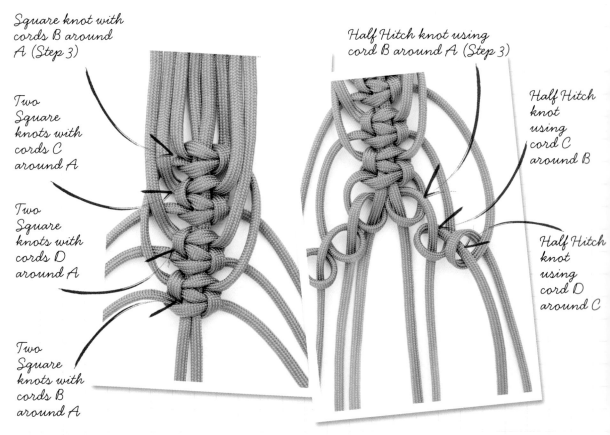

Square knot with cords B around A (Step 3)

Two Square knots with cords C around A

Two Square knots with cords D around A

Two Square knots with cords B around A

Half Hitch knot using cord B around A (Step 3)

Half Hitch knot using cord C around B

Half Hitch knot using cord D around C

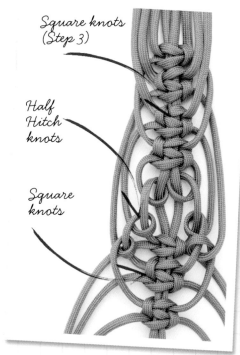

Square knots (Step 3)

Half Hitch knots

Square knots

3   Now repeat this pattern 10 times:
1.   One Square knot (see page 116) using cords B around cords A.
2.   Two Square knots using cords C around cords A.
3.   Two Square knots using cords D around cords A.
4.   Two Square knots using cords B around cords A.
5.   One Half Hitch knot (see page 118) using the left B cord around the left A cord.
6.   One Half Hitch knot using the right B cord around the right A cord.
7.   One Half Hitch knot using the left C cord around the left B cord.
8.   One Half Hitch knot using the right C cord around the right B cord.
9.   One Half Hitch knot using the left D cord around the left C cord.
10. One Half Hitch knot using the right D cord around the right C cord.

4 After 10 repeats, complete only numbers 1-4 in the pattern to end the strap.

5 Cut your piece of leather into four rectangles of 4.5 × 5.5cm (1³⁄₄ × 2in).

6 Remove the pin from the tops of the cords and cover these ends with two of your pieces of leather. Using a sewing machine or superglue, stick the leather pieces and cord ends together. Now make a small hole at the top of the leather using your scissors or the pin. Insert a split ring.

7 Repeat Step 6 at the other end of your strap.

Split ring

Sew or glue two rectangles of leather to the cord ends (Step 6)

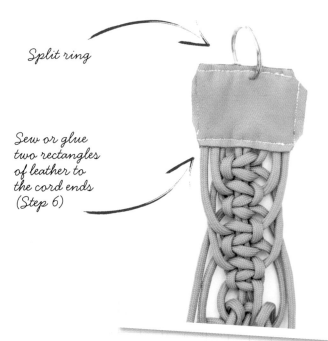

KNOTS NEEDED FOR PROJECT

Josephine knot (see page 120)
Alternating Square knot
(see page 116)
Square knot (see page 116)

MEMO
BOOK™

64 PAGES / MADE IN INDIA

BOTTLE BAG

This piece is perfect for the camper, the festival-goer, the weekend walker or the yogi. The design requires knots of intermediate difficulty that give our bottle bag a modern but outdoorsy feel.

DIMENSIONS
↕ 85cm (33in) maximum

MATERIALS & TOOLS
12m (40ft) of paracord
2 end caps with 8mm (⅓in) diameter
Measuring tape
Scissors
S-hook (optional)
Superglue

INSTRUCTIONS

1 Measure and cut your paracord into these lengths: 4 × 3m (10ft).

2 Using all four lengths and working from the middle of the cords, make a Josephine knot (see page 120).

Josephine knot (Step 2)

Four lengths of paracord

NOTE
Before you tie your Alternating Square knots in Step 3, try hanging the project upside down from an S-hook. This will help you to keep the knots in each row even.

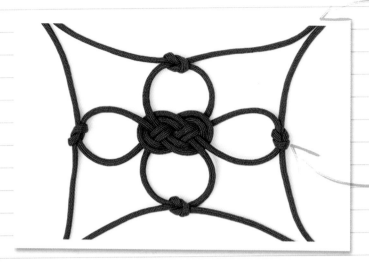

These become the
second row

First row of
Alternating Square
knots completed
(Step 3)

3   Complete five rows of Alternating Square knots (see page
    116), joining each cluster. Leave about 3cm (1¼in) between
each row.

End caps glued into
place (Step 5)

4   Now measure your desired strap length and complete
    a Square knot (see page 116). You are joining all the
lengths of cord together, so that you have two clusters of
four lengths each.

Two clusters of
four lengths each

5   To finish, evenly cut
    the excess cord to
approximately 10cm (4in)
from the Square knot. Glue
the end caps onto the tips of
both clusters.

Square knot
(Step 4)

HOMES & GARDENS PROJECTS

KNOTS NEEDED FOR PROJECT

Chain Sinnet knot (see page 124)

PLACEMAT

Add some handcrafted style to your dining table. Once you've mastered the Chain Sinnet knot, this project is a breeze. The design will also work for mats of any size and shape, from bath mats to floor mats. There is lots of scope for creativity here!

DIMENSIONS
↔ 40cm (16in)
↕ 23cm (9in)

MATERIALS & TOOLS
60m (200ft) of paracord
    for each placemat
Measuring tape
Scissors
Lighter

INSTRUCTIONS

1   Measure and cut your paracord into these lengths:
2 × 22.5m (75ft) in one colour
2 × 7.5m (25ft) in a second colour

2   You will begin working with your two 22.5-m (75-ft) lengths of cord as one. Complete a loose Chain Sinnet knot (see page 124) 40cm (16in) in length.

Working cord

End of cord length

Tying a Chain Sinnet knot (Step 2)

First row of Chain Sinnet knots

3 Once you've completed the 40-cm (16-in) chain, double back and make a second row of chain underneath your first. Ensure you loop through the bottom of the first chain to attach the second row. This technique is very similar to a basic crochet technique.

Second row of Chain Sinnet knots

Working cord

Working cord looped through bottom of the first chain to attach the second row (Step 3)

NOTE
At the end of each row, you may need to add an extra loop to keep an even rectangle shape.

Working cord

Extra loop at the end of the row to keep a rectangular shape

4 Complete 7 rows of Chain Sinnet knots in this way.

5 Take your two 7.5-m (25-ft) lengths of the second colour. Attach to the placemat by melting the ends of the original cords and the new cords together. Complete 3 more rows of Chain Sinnet knots in the second colour.

NOTE
Make sure your Chain Sinnet isn't too tight. The looser it is, the easier it will be to work with.

Cord ends from original and second colours melted together (Step 5)

6 To finish your placemat, cut, melt and press all ends down on the underside. Don't forget your starting ends as well!

Cord ends melted and pressed onto the underside of placemat (Step 6)

NOTE
To give you a rough idea of paracord requirements for mats of different sizes, 122m (400ft) of paracord will make a floor mat of 80 × 45.5cm (31$\frac{1}{2}$ × 18in).

PENDANT LIGHT SHADE

We often forget how beautiful decorative lighting can be and how easily we can use it to create ambience in our homes. This simple project will add character to any space and light up any room.

DIMENSIONS
↕ 20cm (8in)
↔ 16cm (6¼in)

MATERIALS & TOOLS
29m (95ft) of paracord
1 pendant light and globe
Measuring tape
Scissors
Lighter

INSTRUCTIONS

1 Measure and cut your paracord into these lengths:
14 × 2m (6½ft)
1 × 30cm (12in)
1 × 15cm (6in)

Note that, when measuring your last piece of paracord, you will need to match the circumference of your light fitting – yours may be larger or smaller than 15cm (6in). After cutting your cords, melt all the ends with the lighter so that they don't fray.

2 We'll be starting from the bottom of the shade and working upwards. Take the 30-cm (12-in) length and join the ends to create a ring: using a lighter, heat each end and stick them together. This will become the base of the light shade.

3 Fold one of the 2-m (6½-ft) lengths in half and make a Lark's Head knot (see page 115) around the 30-cm (12-in) ring you made in Step 2. Repeat this for the other 13 2-m (6½-ft) lengths.

4 Arrange the 14 Lark's Head knots into clusters of two. With each cluster of two, make a Square Knot (see page 116) about 1.5cm (⅝in) down.

NOTE
When knotting your Alternating Square knots in Step 5, rest the bottom ring over a bowl or your knee. This will make it easier to keep an even shape and ensure that the rows are consistent.

KNOTS NEEDED FOR PROJECT

Lark's Head knot (see page 115)
Square knot (see page 116)
Alternating Square knot
(see page 116)
Overhand knot (see page 115)

5 Now start making Alternating Square knots (see page 116) by linking the clusters together. You can be creative with the shape of the light shade, but if you would like a similar style and form to the pendant shown, follow the pattern below.

Complete seven rows of Alternating Square knots:
- Rows 1 to 3 at 2.5cm (1in) apart
- Rows 3 to 4 at 3cm (1¼in) apart
- Rows 4 to 5 at 3.5cm (1½in) apart
- Rows 5 to 6 at 3cm (1¼in) apart
- Rows 6 to 7 at 2.5cm (1in) apart

NOTE
When creating the ring for the top of the shade in Step 6, you will need to match the circumference of your light fitting. We have used a 15-cm (6-in) length of paracord, but you should measure and cut your paracord accordingly.

6 Now take the 15-cm (6-in) length of paracord and join the ends by melting them with a lighter. This ring will become the top of the light shade.

30-cm (12-in) length of paracord

14 Lark's Head knots grouped into pairs (Step 4)

Make 28 Overhand knots (Step 7)

Leave a 1.5-cm (⅝-in) gap from the last row of Alternating Square knots

7 Flip the light shade so that it is standing on its base. For each length of rope, make an Overhand knot (see page 115) on the 15-cm (6-in) ring, leaving a gap of 1.5cm (⅝in) from the last row of Alternating Square knots. You will be making 28 Overhand knots on the ring.

8 Once all the ends are tied to the top ring, flatten the shade onto its base. You now have easy access to the excess cord. Cut all ends to 3mm (⅛in) long. Heat each end with a lighter and stick it to the inside of the shade by pushing it down with the metal part of your scissors.

9 Stretch the shade back into shape. Thread through the pendant cord and screw in the globe.

Flatten the shade for easy access to the ends (Step 8)

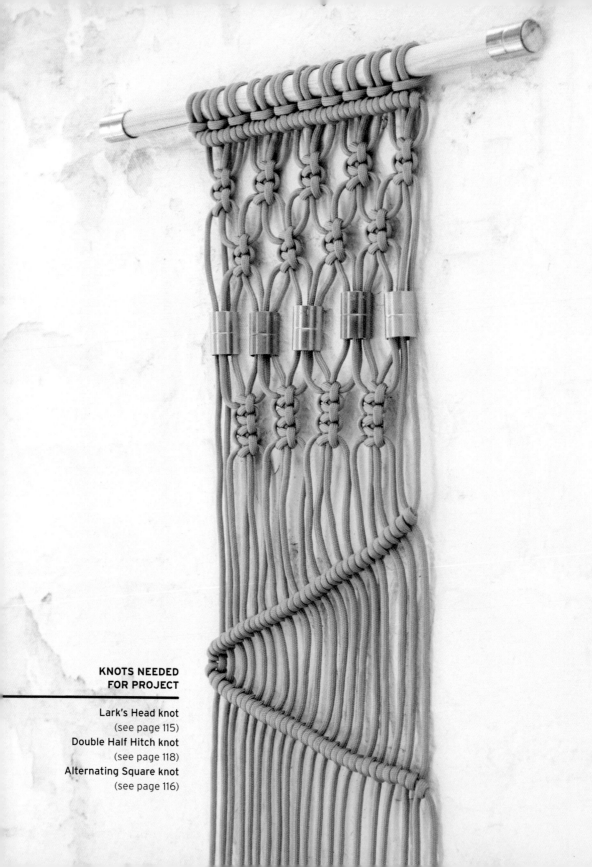

**KNOTS NEEDED
FOR PROJECT**

Lark's Head knot
(see page 115)
Double Half Hitch knot
(see page 118)
Alternating Square knot
(see page 116)

WALL HANGING

Occasionally it's a pleasure to create something that is purely decorative. This project is to craft a beautiful piece of art that you can hang on the wall. The instructions are only a guide – embrace your creativity and let your imagination loose.

DIMENSIONS
↔ 35cm (14in) including dowel
↕ 1m (3ft)

MATERIALS & TOOLS
31m (103ft) of paracord
35cm (14in) dowel with 13mm (½in) diameter
7 copper tubes or similar with 15mm (⅝in) diameter
Measuring tape
Scissors
Lighter
Superglue

INSTRUCTIONS

1 Measure and cut your paracord into these lengths:
1 × 4m (13ft)
9 × 3m (10ft)

2 Using the 4-m (13-ft) length of paracord, make a Lark's Head knot (see page 115) at the left end of the dowel. Do not make your knot exactly in the middle of the cord: the left length of cord should be 2.5m (8ft) long and the right length 1.5m (5ft) long.

3 Attach each of the nine 3-m (10-ft) cords to the dowel using the Lark's Head knot. This time, do make your knots in the middle of the cords, so that they have equal lengths on the left and right. Space your cords evenly along the dowel.

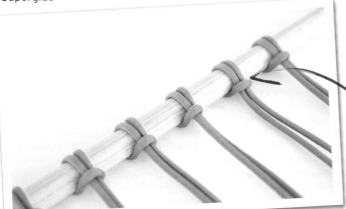

Lark's Head knots (Step 3)

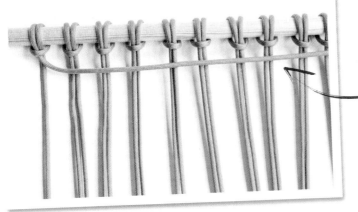

Lay the longer 2.5-m (8-ft) cord across the others (Step 4)

4 Take the longer 2.5-m (8-ft) length of cord on the far left of the piece. Lay it across all the other cords. Working from the left, make a row of Double Half Hitch knots (see page 118) around the longer cord.

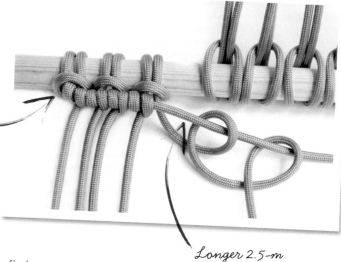

Working from the left, make a row of Double Half Hitch knots (Step 4)

Longer 2.5-m (8-ft) cord

5 Divide your twenty cords into five groups of four. Now make two rows of Alternating Square knots (see page 116), with two square knots in each cluster. You will have five clusters in your first row and four clusters in your second row.

6 Again divide your twenty cords into five groups of four. Make another row of Alternating Square knots with just one square knot in each cluster.

7 Take five of the copper tubes and thread each cluster through, covering the last row of Alternating Square knots. The knots will help the tubes to stay in place.

NOTE
You can easily customise this design to include other knots and patterns of your choice.

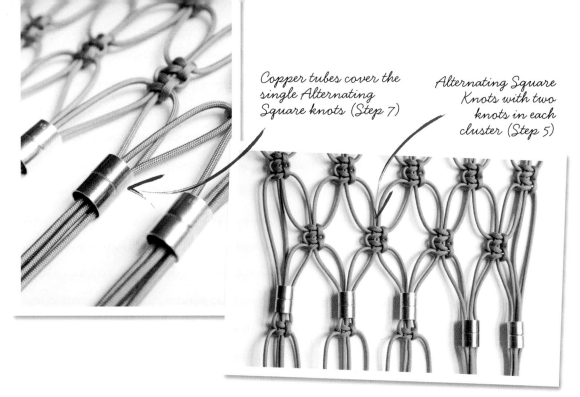

Copper tubes cover the single Alternating Square knots (Step 7)

Alternating Square Knots with two knots in each cluster (Step 5)

8 Now make one last row of Alternating Square knots with three square knots in each cluster.

9 Take the right outermost cord (the longer length). Lay it diagonally across the piece. Working from the right, make a diagonal line of Double Half Hitch knots around the longer length.

10 Once you have reached the end, make another diagonal line of Double Half Hitch knots, this time working from left to right. When you have finished this second line, you will have made an arrow, or zigzag shape with your two lines of Double Half Hitch knots.

11 Cut all the remaining cord to your desired tassel length. Using the lighter, burn each of the ends to stop them from fraying.

12 Superglue the last two copper tubes to the ends of the dowel.

Diagonal line of Double Half Hitch knots (Step 9)

PLANT HANGER

Indoor plants fill our homes with life and there's no better presentation than a handmade macramé plant hanger. This project takes some effort, but the end result is worth every second.

DIMENSIONS

↕ 80–130cm (30–50in)

MATERIALS & TOOLS

42m (134½ft) of paracord
1 medium wooden ring or
    similar
Measuring tape
Scissors
S-hook (optional)
Lighter

INSTRUCTIONS

1   Measure and cut your paracord into these lengths:
8 × 5m (16ft).
Keep the excess 2m (6½ft) of cord to one side for now.

2   Take all eight lengths of cord and thread them through the wooden ring until it is in the middle.

3   Using a piece of your excess cord, make a Wrapping knot (see page 119) around all the lengths just below the ring. Make sure you pull the knot through, so that it's hidden underneath the wrapped cord. Cut off the excess cord and push the ends inside as well.

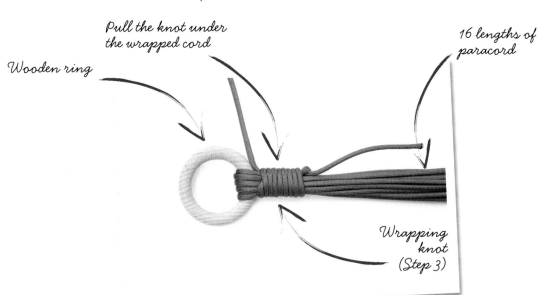

Pull the knot under the wrapped cord

16 lengths of paracord

Wooden ring

Wrapping knot (Step 3)

KNOTS NEEDED FOR PROJECT

Wrapping knot (see page 119)
Square knot (see page 116)
Half Hitch knot (see page 118)
Alternating Square knot (see
page 116)

4 Now you have 16 lengths of paracord to work with. Group these into four clusters of four.

5 Now you will work on each cluster independently. For each cluster, complete the knot pattern on the bottom right.

Three Square knots (Step 5)

Four-finger gap

Half Hitch knot with cords 1 and 2 around 3 and 4

Half Hitch knot with cords 3 and 4 around 1 and 2

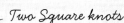

1 2 3 4

Four-finger gap (Step 5)

Two Square knots

Two-finger gap

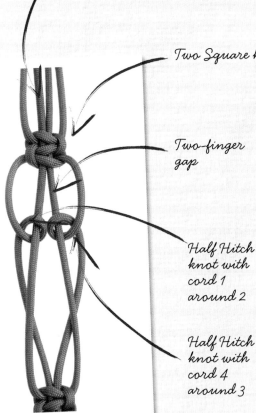

Half Hitch knot with cord 1 around 2

Half Hitch knot with cord 4 around 3

- Three Square knots (see page 116).
- Leave a four-finger gap.
- One Half Hitch knot (see page 118) with cords 1 and 2 around 3 and 4.
- One Half Hitch knot with cords 3 and 4 around 1 and 2.
- Leave a four-finger gap.
- Two Square knots.
- Leave a two-finger gap.
- One Half Hitch knot with cord 1 around 2 and, beside it, one Half Hitch knot with cord 4 around 3.
- Leave a four-finger gap.
- Twist over cord 1 with cord 2, and cord 3 with cord 4.
- Five Square knots.
- Leave a four-finger gap.
- One Half Hitch knot with cords 1 and 2 around 3 and 4.
- One Half Hitch knot with cords 3 and 4 around 1 and 2.

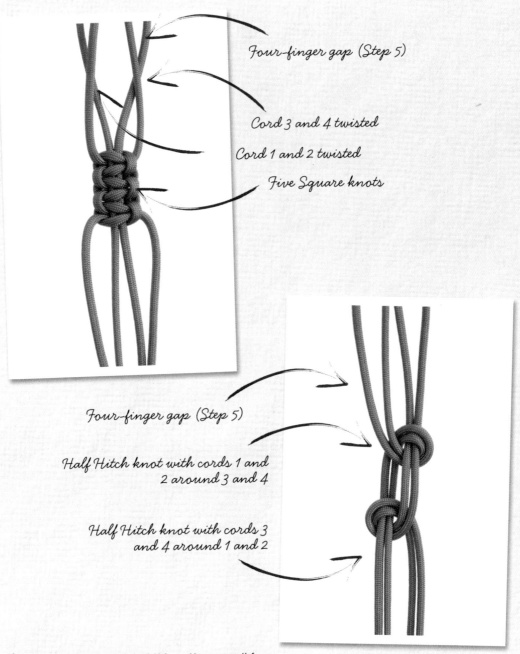

Four-finger gap (Step 5)

Cord 3 and 4 twisted

Cord 1 and 2 twisted

Five Square knots

Four-finger gap (Step 5)

Half Hitch knot with cords 1 and 2 around 3 and 4

Half Hitch knot with cords 3 and 4 around 1 and 2

6 Once you've completed this pattern on all four clusters, complete three rows of Alternating Square knots (see page 116), leaving a gap of approximately 5cm (2in) between each row.

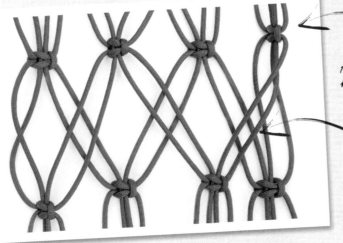

Alternating Square knots (Step 6)

5cm (2in) between each row

7 Using another piece of excess cord, make a Wrapping knot around all 16 lengths, approximately 5cm (2in) below the last row of Alternating Square knots. Cut and hide any excess cord inside the knot.

8 To finish, trim all 16 cords to your desired tassel length. Cleanly melt the ends to prevent fraying.

Wrapping knot around all 16 lengths (Step 7)

Ends hidden inside the knot

NOTE
It's easier to work vertically on this project, so try hanging it from an S-hook. While working on one of your clusters in Step 5, hang the other clusters over the hook so that they're out of your working space.

KNOTS NEEDED FOR PROJECT

Crown knot (see page 122)
Eight-Strand Diamond Braid
knot (see page 127)

GUIDED LONDON

POTS & COASTERS

This project provides you with the freedom to craft endless varieties of pots, coasters and plates. Whether you're making a pen holder, fruit bowl or even a washing basket, let your imagination loose!

DIMENSIONS

Coaster
↔ 14cm (5½in) diameter
Pot
↕ 9cm (3½in) tall

MATERIALS & TOOLS

10m (32ft) of paracord for
    each pot or coaster
1 metal end cap with 15mm
    (⅝in) diameter
    (optional)
Measuring tape
Scissors
Lighter
Superglue

INSTRUCTIONS

1 Measure and cut your paracord into these lengths:
4 × 2.5m (8ft).

2 Divide the paracord lengths into two clusters of two. Working in the middle of your lengths, make a Crown knot (see page 122).

3 You now have eight lengths of paracord to work with. Complete an Eight-Strand Diamond Braid (see page 127) along the whole length of the cords.

Crown knot (Step 2)

Eight-Strand
Diamond
Braid knot
(Step 3)

NOTE
The paracord measurements given here are for making the small coasters and pots pictured. 20m (65½ft) of paracord will make a bowl that is 18cm (7in) tall with a diameter of 28cm (11in).

4 Evenly cut your ends, then melt them all together. Use the blunt inside edge of your scissor handles to clamp them together.

5 Now coil the rope around your Crown knot three times, using superglue to stick each coil to the previous one as you work.

CONTINUE TO MAKE A COASTER

6 Finish coiling the rope round and round, gluing as you go. When you have used up all your rope, you can either glue on an end cap or weave the melted end into the underside of the coaster and stick it with superglue.

Superglue between coils

Three coils of rope (Step 5)

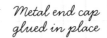
Metal end cap glued in place

Coils glued together, working into a pot shape (Pot Step 6)

NOTE
When coiling your pot, work around a bottle or bowl with the shape you want to achieve. This will help you coil the rope up evenly.

CONTINUE TO MAKE A POT

6 After completing your three base coils, start to coil the remaining rope upwards, working into a pot shape. Superglue each coil to the previous one.

7 Once you've finished coiling the rope, glue on a metal end cap, or weave the melted end into the pot and stick it inside with superglue. Make sure it's well hidden.

HANGING TABLE

Beautiful, practical, simple and modern, this hanging side table will add a designer touch to any room. You'll have no trouble crafting this timeless piece with traditional macramé knots and just a few additional materials.

DIMENSIONS

↔ 25cm (10in) diameter
↕ 120cm (4ft) maximum

MATERIALS & TOOLS

1 round plastic mould 25cm
    (10in) in diameter and
    2cm (³⁄₄in) high or similar
3 plastic tubes with 6mm
    (¼in) diameter and
    longer than the mould
    height
Cooking oil
2.5kg (5½lb) of cement
19m (62ft) of paracord
1 medium split ring
Cling film
Measuring tape
Superglue
Scissors
Lighter

Superglue the tubes into the mould in a perfect triangle, 2.5cm (1in) from the edge (Step 1)

INSTRUCTIONS

FOR MAKING THE CEMENT TABLE BASE

1 Measure and mark the points of a perfect triangle, 2.5cm (1in) from the edge of the plastic mould. Superglue the three plastic tubes onto your marked points, ends up.

2 Coat the entire mould (including the tubes) in cooking oil. This will help you remove the dried cement from the mould and give the table top a smooth finish.

3 Mix your cement according to the instructions on the packet.

Flexible plastic mould

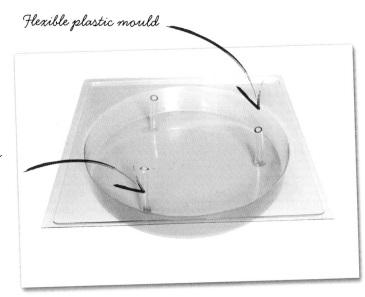

KNOTS NEEDED FOR PROJECT

Wrapping knot (see page 119)
Half Hitch knot (see page 118)
Square knot (see page 116)
Overhand knot (see page 115)

NOTE
Plastic moulds can be bought
online from garden supply,
hardware or craft shops Your
mould should be slightly flexible
to help you press out your table
base once the cement has set.

Cover with cling film to keep the cement clean as it dries

4 Pour the cement slowly into the mould. Tap the mould on the ground a few times to remove any air bubbles. Continue tapping until the top of the cement is reasonably smooth. Cover the mould with cling film to keep the cement clean as it dries.

5 Leave the cement to dry as described in the instructions on your cement packet. This will be at least 24 hours.

6 Once the cement is dry, tip the mould upside down and gently push the slab out. The tubes may detach as you do this; if they do not, just pull them out.

NOTE
Remember to mix up more cement if you are using a mould larger than the 25cm (10in) diameter mould pictured here.

ADDING PARACORD

7 Measure and cut your paracord into these lengths:

3 × 4m (13ft)
3 × 2m (6½ft)

Keep the excess cord to one side for now.

8 Take the three 4-m (13-ft) lengths of paracord and thread them through the split ring until it is in the middle. Now take the three 2-m (6½-ft) lengths and thread them through the ring until about 5cm (2in) hangs over the ring.

9 Using a piece of excess cord, make a Wrapping knot (see page 119) around all the cords just below the ring. This will secure and hide the short ends of the three 2-m (6½-ft) lengths. Hide the knot under the wrapped cord. Cut off the ends and hide those inside as well.

10 You now have nine lengths of paracord to work with. Group these into three clusters of three.

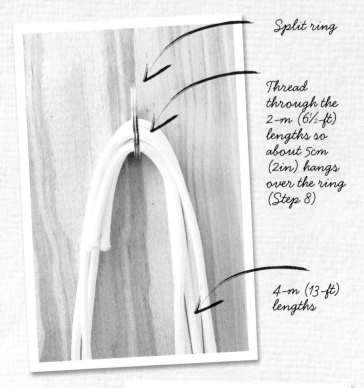

Split ring

Thread through the 2-m (6½-ft) lengths so about 5cm (2in) hangs over the ring (Step 8)

4-m (13-ft) lengths

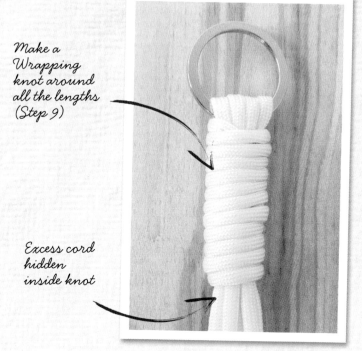

Make a Wrapping knot around all the lengths (Step 9)

Excess cord hidden inside knot

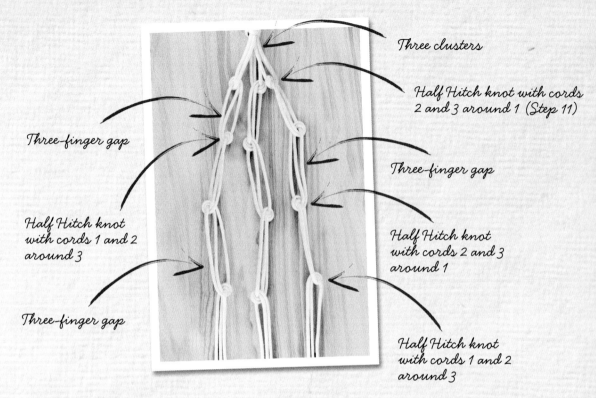

Three clusters

Half Hitch knot with cords 2 and 3 around 1 (Step 11)

Three-finger gap

Three-finger gap

Half Hitch knot with cords 1 and 2 around 3

Half Hitch knot with cords 2 and 3 around 1

Three-finger gap

Half Hitch knot with cords 1 and 2 around 3

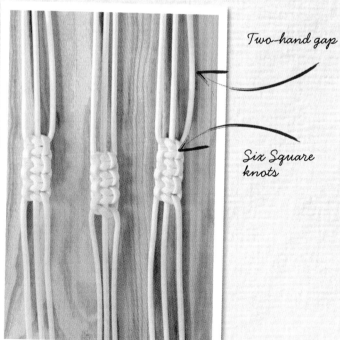

Two-hand gap

Six Square knots

11 You will be working on each cluster independently. For each cluster, complete this knot pattern:

- One Half Hitch knot (see pgae 118) with cords 2 and 3 around 1.
- Leave a three-finger gap.
- One Half Hitch knot with cords 1 and 2 around 3.
- Leave a three-finger gap.
- One Half Hitch knot with cords 2 and 3 around 1.
- Leave a three-finger gap.
- One Half Hitch knot with cords 1 and 2 around 3.
- Leave a two-hand gap.
- Six Square knots (see page 116).

12 Once you have completed the pattern with all three clusters, take your cement base and thread each rope cluster through its individual hole.

13 To finish, make an Overhand knot (see page 115) on each cluster, underneath the cement base. Cut your ends evenly, then melt them to stop them from fraying.

(see page 115)

NOTE
You may need to adjust the Overhand knots underneath the base to make the table level.

Thread each cluster through a hole in the cement base (Step 12)

Tie an Overhand knot (Step 13)

Ends evenly cut and melted

CHAIR

If you have a couple of old lawn chairs or chair frames in your garage, pull them out and give them a whole new lease of life. You have creative licence to go wild with your colours and patterns. This is the perfect project for a summer's day.

DIMENSIONS
↕ This pattern fits a chair 75cm (30in) tall

MATERIALS & TOOLS
180m (590ft) of paracord in the colours of your choice
1 lawn chair frame
2 crochet hooks or pens of 1cm (³/₈in) diameter minimum
1 macramé chair pattern (supplied on page 98)
Scissors
Lighter
Measuring tape

KNOTS NEEDED FOR PROJECT
Square knot (see page 116)
Chain Sinnet knot (see page 124)

INSTRUCTIONS

1 This project is based upon a macramé weaving pattern of 39 vertical knots and 38 horizontal knots, which will fit a chair 75cm (30in) tall. The following measurements may need to change, depending on your frame size, pattern and colours. To follow this pattern exactly, measure and cut your paracord into these lengths:

1 × 90m (295ft)
4 × 22m (72ft) in different colours

2 Remove any material covering the chair frame, leaving just the skeleton.

Chair frame measuring 75cm (30in) tall

DESIGN TEMPLATES

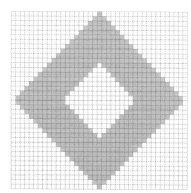

Seat pattern

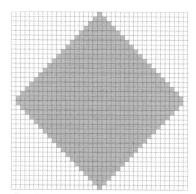

Back pattern

These design templates can be used to replicate the pattern on this chair. The grey squares show where the coloured cord is woven over the vertical white cords. Follow this pattern or get creative and come up with your own unique design to suit your style.

3 First we will knot the vertical cords. Position your 90-m (295-ft) length of paracord under the seat of the chair. Leaving approximately 5cm (2in) of cord at the end, make a tight double Square knot (see page 116) underneath the bottom left corner of the chair seat. Make your knot on the straight edge of the chair frame: don't try to knot on any round corners.

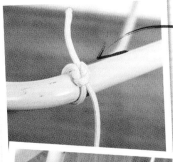

Make a double Square knot on the bottom left corner of the chair frame (Step 3)

Take your working cord under the centre bar, then up and over the top of the frame (Step 4)

4 Now take your working cord under the centre bar, then up and over the top of the frame. Make a loop and wrap the loop around the top bar, ending on the left-hand side.

Make a loop (Step 4)

Wrap the loop around the top bar, ending on the left-hand side (Step 4)

5 Place one of your crochet hooks or pens inside the loop you just created. Pull the cord tight so that the hook/pen stays in place. This knotting technique uses the Chain Sinnet knot (see page 124).

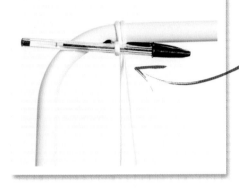

Place a pen or crochet hook inside the loop (Step 5) and pull the cord tight so that the pen or hook stays in place

6 Now take the working cord back down, under the centre bar, then up and over the bottom bar. Make a loop and wrap it around the bar to the left, wrapping around the Square knot already there. Then place your second hook or pen inside the loop.

Take the working cord back down, under the centre bar (Step 6)

NOTE
It is easiest to work with a crochet hook when pulling one loop through another. If you're working with a pen or pencil, as shown here, gradually remove your pen from loop A while replacing it with loop B, so that the second loop slips easily through the first.

Take the working cord over the bottom bar, then make a loop (Step 6)

Wrap the loop around the bar to the left, around the Square knot (Step 6)

Place a pen or crochet hook inside the loop and pull the cord tight (Step 6)

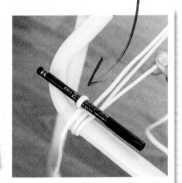

7 Again take your working cord under the centre bar, then up and over the top of the frame. Make a loop and wrap it around the top bar. Make sure that the loop comes round on the left-hand side of the cord. Let's call this second loop, loop B.

Take the working cord under the centre bar, then over the top of the frame again (Step 7)

Make a loop (Step 7)

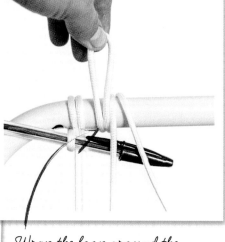

Wrap the loop around the top bar, coming round to the left-hand side of the cord (Step 7)

8 If you're using a crochet hook, you can just hook around loop B and pull it through loop A.

If you're using a pen or pencil, then simply remove it from loop A and thread loop B through loop A. Insert the crochet hook/pen in the remaining loop.

Pull loop B through loop A (Step 8)

Put your pencil or crochet hook into the remaining loop (Step 8)

9 Repeat Steps 7 and 8, going up and down the entire width of your chair. My pattern uses 39 vertical pairs of knots, but yours may need a different number.

If working with a pen, gradually remove it from loop A while replacing it with loop B

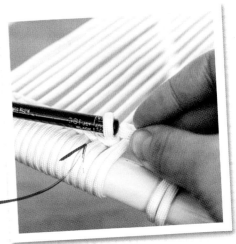

Pull the working cord over the bottom bar, then pull loop B through loop A

Repeat the pattern along the width of the frame (Step 9) Always put your pen or crochet hook in the remaining loop

10 When you are ready to make the last knot on the top bar of the frame, measure and cut your working cord so that it is long enough to make the final pass. Then pull the working cord all the way through the final top loop.

On the final knot on the top bar, pull the working cord all the way through the loop (Step 10)

11 For the last time, take the working cord back down, under the centre bar then up and over the bottom bar. Loop around the bottom bar and thread the loops into each other. Then, as you just did on the top bar, pull the working cord all the way through the loop.

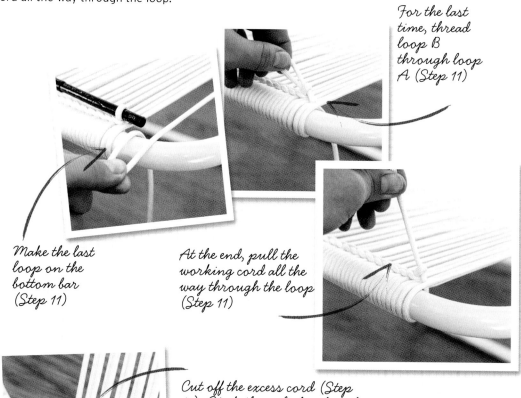

For the last time, thread loop B through loop A (Step 11)

Make the last loop on the bottom bar (Step 11)

At the end, pull the working cord all the way through the loop (Step 11)

Cut off the excess cord (Step 12). Stick the melted end to the underside of the chair

The vertical knots are completed (Step 12)

12 To tie off the cord, make a tight double Square knot under the chair, as you did at the beginning. Cut the excess cords to around 2.5cm (1in), then melt and press them both down to the underside of the chair. Make sure they stick well. You've now completed all the vertical knots for your chair.

13 Now we will complete the horizontal knotting and weaving. You will follow the process in Steps 3 to 12, this time working horizontally, from the bottom of the left-hand bar to the top of the right bar. Attach your first cord by making a tight double Square knot.

To start your horizontal weaving, make a tight double Square knot (Step 13)

14 To create your design, weave your coloured cord in and out of the vertical cords according to your pattern. You can make your own pattern, find one or use mine.

Pass your cord in front of or behind the vertical cords according to your pattern (Step 14)

15 As when making your vertical knots, always wrap up and over each bar. Loop around the bar, ensuring that you're always looping the cord to the left, or towards the beginning. Always thread loop B through loop A to create your chain.

16 On the final pass (for both the back of the chair and the seat), pull the working end all the way through the last loops. To tie off the cord, make a double Square knot, then cut and melt the excess cord.

As before, use a pen or crochet hook in your loops (Step 15)

Your pattern starts to take shape (Step 15)

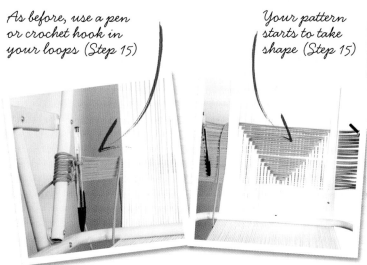

Change colours here so that the connection is hidden

HAMMOCK

There is no better place to relax than in your own handmade hammock. This design requires just one easy, repeated knot, so it makes a perfectly simple but thoroughly satisfying project.

DIMENSIONS
↕ 4m (13ft)
↔ 1m (3ft)

MATERIALS & TOOLS
144m (480ft) of paracord
Measuring tape
Scissors
Lighter

INSTRUCTIONS

1 Measure and cut your paracord into these lengths:
24 × 6m (20ft)
Melt the ends with a lighter so that they don't fray.

2 Gather all the 24 lengths at one end. Tie them together using an Overhand knot (see page 115) about 30cm (1ft) from their ends.

Tie an Overhand knot, leaving 30cm (1ft) at the ends (Step 2)

24 lengths

NOTE
When making your rows of Overhand knots, ensure that your knots are tight and level with each other.

KNOTS NEEDED FOR PROJECT

Overhand knot (see page 115)

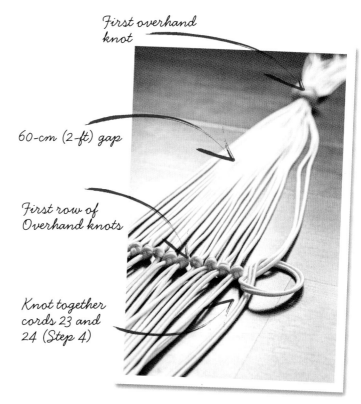

3 Lay your piece on a flat
surface to start knotting your
pattern. Leave a 60-cm (2-ft) gap
below the Overhand knot before
beginning your first row of knots.

60-cm (2-ft) gap

4 Working from the left-hand
cord, knot together the first
two cords – cords 1 and 2 – using
an Overhand knot. Repeat this for
cords 3 and 4, 5 and 6 and so on,
until you have made 12 Overhand
knots in a row.

*First row of
Overhand knots*

*Knot together
cords 23 and
24 (Step 4)*

*Skip cords 1 and 24 on
every second row (Step 5)*

5 Leave a 7.5-cm (3-in) gap before starting
your second row of knots. Work from the left
again. This time, skip cord 1 and instead tie
together cords 2 and 3, 4 and 5 and so on. Skip
cord 24. Leave another 7.5-cm (3-in) gap before
beginning your next row.

6 Repeat Steps 4 and 5 until you have
approximately 1m (3ft) of cord remaining.
Make sure your last row includes cords 1 and 24.

*Leave a 7.5-cm (3-in) gap
between rows*

7 Now make a large Overhand knot with all 24 lengths, leaving a 60-cm (2-ft) gap from your final row of knots.

8 Cut and melt the excess cords to match your other end.

KNOTS OPTIONAL FOR PROJECT

Josephine knot (see page 120)
or
Carrick Bend knot (see page 120)

VASE COVERING

With this quick and easy project, you can turn glass jars or unwanted old vases into eye-catching, colourful pieces. It is also a great way to recycle your scrap paracord.

DIMENSIONS
Various

MATERIALS & TOOLS
2m (6½ft) of paracord in the colours of your choice
1 old vase or jar
Measuring tape
Scissors
Lighter
Superglue

INSTRUCTIONS

1 Measure and cut a length of paracord:
1 x 2m (6½ft).
You will need more paracord if you are decorating a large vase. You might choose to cut two or more different colours. Melt the starting end of the paracord to stop it from fraying.

2 Using superglue, stick the end of the paracord onto the vase. Start wrapping the cord around the vase as many times as you desire.

3 If you want to have two (or more) colours, melt and join the ends of your new colour and the old colour, then continue wrapping.

4 To finish, melt the end of the paracord and superglue it to the vase.

5 (optional) Make a Josephine knot (see page 120) or Carrick Bend knot (see page 120). Finish the knot cleanly by cutting the excess cords and melting them to the underside. Superglue the knot onto the front of the vase.

NOTE
If you are changing paracord colour, make the join on the same side of the vase as you started wrapping.

ELECTRIC CORD COVERING

Upgrade your dull desk lamp or pendant light with a simple macramé Half knot. This project is a very easy way to craft something old into something beautifully new.

DIMENSIONS
↕ 1.5m (5ft)

MATERIALS & TOOLS
3m (10ft) of paracord
1 old lamp, pendant light or
    anything with a cord
Measuring tape
Scissors
Lighter

INSTRUCTIONS

1 Measure and cut a length of paracord:
1 × 3m (10ft).
You will need more paracord to cover a longer electric cord. You might choose to cut two or more colours.

2 Working around your electric cord, make a Half knot (see page 117) in the middle of the length of paracord.

3 Continue making Half knots for the entire length of your electric cord.

4 To finish, cut and melt the two ends of paracord together.

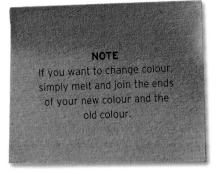

NOTE
If you want to change colour, simply melt and join the ends of your new colour and the old colour.

CAUTION
Always be careful when working with electrical appliances. Unplug the lamp before you begin this project and be very careful not to melt the plastic of the electric cord when you melt the ends of the paracord together.

KNOTS NEEDED FOR PROJECT

Half knot (see page 117)

KNOTS NEEDED FOR PROJECT

Four-Strand Diamond
Braid knot (see page 127)
Wrapping knot (see page 119)

DOG LEAD

If your dog's lead is looking old and frayed, this über-easy project will provide you with a new one. In no time at all, you'll be running your dog around the park with a brand-new look.

DIMENSIONS
↕ 95cm (38in)

MATERIALS & TOOLS
7m (24ft) of paracord
1 clasp or clip
Embroidery thread
Measuring tape
Scissors
Lighter

INSTRUCTIONS

1 Measure and cut your paracord into these lengths: 4 × 1.75m (6ft).

2 Take all four lengths of paracord and, using the lighter, melt the ends together to make just one end.

3 Now start to make a Four-Strand Diamond Braid knot (see page 127). When your braid reaches 33cm (13in) long, curl it around to make a large loop (this will become the handle). Weave the working ends through the beginning of the braid twice.

4 Continue the Four-Strand Diamond Braid knot for another 80cm (32in).

5 Thread your clasp or clip onto the lead. Now curl the braid around to create a small loop with the clasp/clip inside. Weave the working ends into the completed braid twice, just as you did in Step 3.

6 Cut and melt these ends together.

7 Using embroidery thread, make a Wrapping knot (see page 119) around both connecting sections to cover the melted cords. Make sure you tie and hide the ends of the thread, so that it doesn't unravel.

Weave the working ends through the beginning of the braid twice (Step 3)

Melted starting ends

THE KNOTS

OVERHAND KNOT

The commonly used Overhand knot is very easy to form and extremely strong when complete. It's often used to bind two cords together, as shown in the photo, left.

1   Make a loop with your length(s) of rope.
2   Pass one end around and through the loop.
3   Pull both ends to tighten.

LARK'S HEAD KNOT

This simple knot is traditionally used at the beginning of a macramé piece to attach a cord length to a rod, buckle or another cord. To demonstrate it, we will work with two cords.

1   Arrange the cords so that one is horizontal at the top – this is the holding cord. Fold the second cord in half with a loop at the top.
2   Pass the loop behind and around the holding cord.
3   Then pass the loose ends of the working cord through the loop that is now in front of the holding cord.
4   Pull the loose ends to tighten the knot.

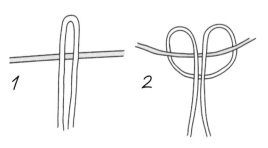

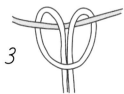

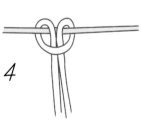

SQUARE KNOT

The Square knot is also known as a Reef or Flat knot. Square knots are tied with two cords working over any number of holding cords (usually two).

1 Arrange the cords so that the two working cords are on the outside and the holding cords are in the centre. Take the left-hand working cord over the two holding cords and underneath the right-hand cord.

2 Take the right-hand cord under the two holding cords and up through the loop created on the left-hand side.

3 Take the right-hand cord over the two holding cords and under the left-hand cord.

4 Take the left-hand cord under the two holding cords and up through the loop on the right-hand side. Pull the tails of the cords to tighten the knot. This completes one Square knot.

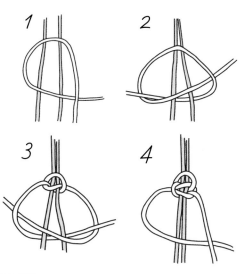

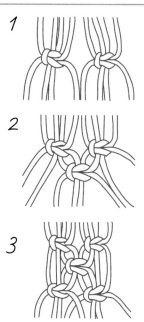

ALTERNATING SQUARE KNOT

The Alternating Square Knot is a pattern of Square knots (see above), using eight cords or more.

1 If working with eight cords, divide them into two groups of four. (If working with 12 cords, as in the photograph, right, divide them into three groups of four.) In each group, tie a Square knot with the two outer cords over the two centre cords.

2 Bring the two left-hand cords of the right group and the two right-hand cords of the left group to the centre, dropping the two outer cords on each side. In your central group, tie a Square knot with the two outer cords over the two centre cords.

HALF KNOT

This knot is the first half of the Square knot (see page 116), tied repeatedly in a chain to create an attractive spiral knot. Approximately eight knots are required to complete a twist. You will be working with two lengths of paracord, each folded in half.

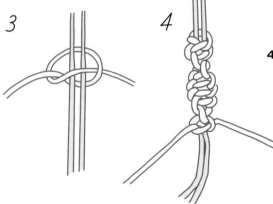

1   Arrange the cords so that the two working cords are on the outside. The two middle cords are the holding cords that the knot will be tied around (these holding cords could be any material, not just paracord!).

2   Pass the left-hand cord over the two holding cords and under the right-hand cord.

3   Now take the right-hand cord under the two holding cords and through the loop created on the left-hand side. Pull the cords to tighten.

4   Repeat Steps 2 and 3 until the knotting is at your desired length. The tighter these knots are, the more attractive the pattern will be.

3   You have now completed one unit of the Alternating Square knot. To continue the pattern, create a Square knot with your four left-hand cords and then with your four right-hand cords.

4   Repeat Steps 2 and 3 until you've reached the desired length.

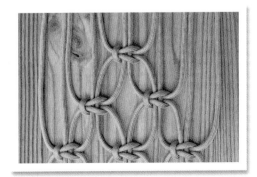

SINGLE AND DOUBLE HALF HITCH

This knot is a very versatile macramé knot. It can be tied vertically, horizontally, diagonally, from right to left and vice versa. It is also known as the Clove Hitch.

SINGLE

1 To create a vertical Half Hitch, arrange two cords parallel to each other. Make a loop with the left-hand cord around the right-hand cord: taking the working end of the left-hand cord behind, over, under and back through the loop.

VERTICAL DOUBLE

2 To create a vertical Double Half Hitch, arrange four (or more) separate cords parallel to one another. Create a loop with the left-hand cord around the cord next to it.

3 Create a second loop to complete the Double Half Hitch. Make another Double Half Hitch around the next cord, looping the same left-hand cord. Repeat with all the cords, until you get to the right-hand cord, then return in the same way to the left-hand side.

HORIZONTAL AND DIAGONAL DOUBLE

4 To create a horizontal Double Half Hitch, arrange the cords as in Step 1, but pass the left-hand one across the others. This is the knot bearer and the Double Half Hitches are tied around this cord.

5 Loop each cord twice around the knot-bearing cord. When you get to the last cord on the right, loop the knot-bearing cord back towards the left and continue as before.

6 Diagonal Double Half Hitch can be tied in the same way as the horizontal Double Half Hitches, simply lay your knot-bearing cord diagonally across the others.

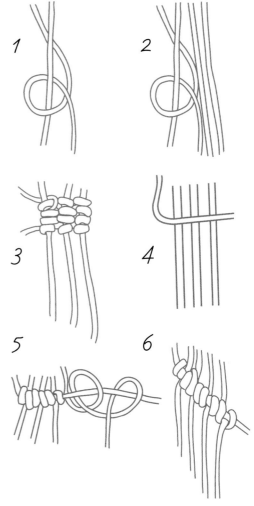

Diagonal Double Half Hitch knot

SLIDE KNOT

The Slide knot is perfect for threading through jewellery ends and finishing off necklaces, as the knot can be moved up and down the cord to alter its length.

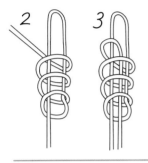

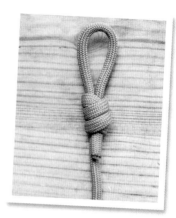

1   First, take your cord and make a loop.
2   Now coil one end of the cord around the loop three times.
3   To finish, thread the working end though the centre of the coil.
4   Pull tight.

WRAPPING KNOT

A frequently used knot in the macramé world, the Wrapping knot decoratively gathers a number of cords together in one bundle. It's simple to create and a very nice knot to start or complete a project.

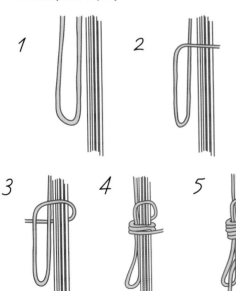

1   Gather all your lengths of cord together. Make a loop with another length of cord (or thread). Make sure this length is long enough to complete the number of wraps you desire.
2   Cross the left end of the loop over the right end and the gathered lengths.
3   Begin to wrap this working end around all the cord lengths and the loop itself.
4   Repeat the wrapping until you reach your desired number.
5   To finish, pass the working cord through the loop at the bottom. Pull both ends until the knot is tight. Then pull the top cord until the knot slips and disappears under the wraps. Cut both ends and hide them under the wraps.

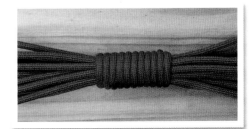

JOSEPHINE KNOT

This macramé knot is also known as the Chinese knot. It is similar to the Carrick Bend knot (see below), but uses two cords rather than one.

1   Make a loop with cord A, passing the cord under itself to create the loop, as shown.
2   Make a second loop with cord B, passing it through the first loop as shown. Ensure that you follow the pattern of overs and unders exactly.
3   To double the knot (which will make it more stable), add two further cords. Feed through the two extra cords, following the pattern of first cord A and then cord B. Ensure that the second pattern lies parallel to the first, with no twists. You can even add a fifth and sixth cord to triple the knot as shown in the photograph above. Pull the cords gently to tighten the knot.

CARRICK BEND KNOT

This is a lovely decorative knot that can be left flat, known as the Carrick Bend mat, or pulled tight to form a more practical knot. You will be working with one cord.

1   Create two loops with the cord, ensuring that the overs and unders are as shown.
2   Make another loop, ensuring that the working cord goes under, over, under, over and under as shown.
3   Continue looping the cord round to create a fourth loop and follow the original pattern to begin doubling the knot.
4   Continue following the knotting around a second or third time to finish the knot. Make sure each repeat lies parallel to the first, with no crossovers of the cord.

TURK'S HEAD KNOT

This knot creates a multi-strand braid pattern, but uses only one cord. You can knot around different-sized tubes to craft variations in knot circumference.

1   Make a loop around the tube, crossing over the cord at the front.
2   Bring the cord back to the front, then weave the working cord from right to left, over the first loop and under the second.
3   Now pull the right-hand loop over the left-hand loop, creating new loops.
4   Take the working cord end and weave it from left to right, going over the first loop and then under the second loop.
5   Pull the left-hand loop over the right-hand loop.
6   Now repeat Steps 2–5 until the cord is back at the starting point.
7   Complete the braid by following the original pattern around a second and third time to create a three-strand braid.

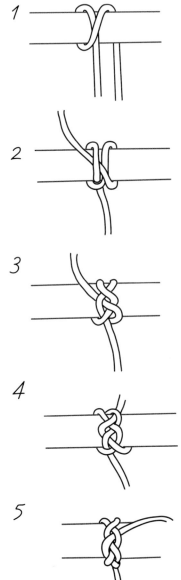

CROWN KNOT

This is a pretty connecting knot that is completed with two or more cords. Although its appearance changes slightly with a greater number of cords, the technique is the same. It is often completed at the end of another knot.

1   Take two or more cords and overlap them in the middle.
2   Take one side of the bottom cord and, in a clockwise direction, cross it over the next cord.
3   Still working in a clockwise direction, take the cord you just crossed over and cross it over the next cord.
4   Repeat Step 3 with the next cord, and so on.
5   When you're on the final cord, thread it through the loop of the first cord.
6   Pull all cords tight, so you have a nice, clean knot.

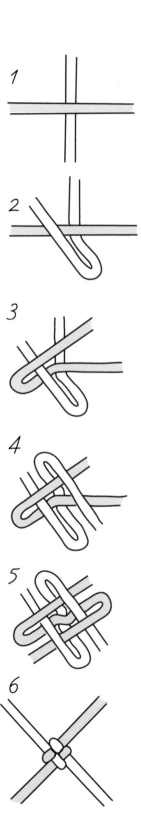

GLOBE KNOT

The Globe knot gets its name from its perfectly round shape. You will need a small ball (wooden or metal) to insert in this knot, as well as a rod – such as a wooden dowel – to help you complete it.

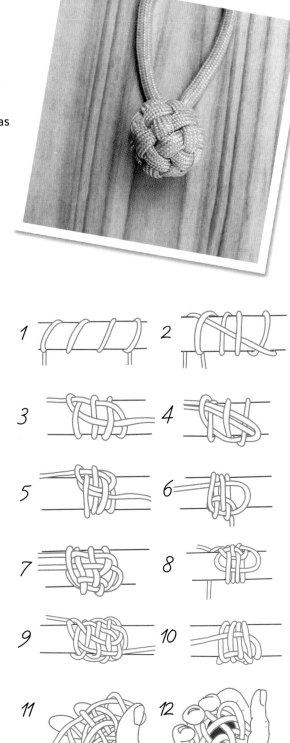

1   Wrap a length of cord around the rod four times, leaving plenty of cord at both ends.
2   Weave the right-hand working end along the rod towards the left: take it over the right-hand coil, under the next coil, over the next coil and under the final one.
3   Now weave the left-hand working end towards the right, passing below the cord you have just woven. Pass the cord under the first coil, over the second, under the third and over the final one.
4   Using the working end on the right, double the top weave: pass it over, under, over and under the coils.
5   Double the bottom weave using the bottom left cord: pass it under, over, under and over the coils.
6   Spread the two top cords apart.
7   Weave the right cord between the two top cords.
8   Spread the bottom two cords apart.
9   Weave the bottom left cord under and over to the right.
10 Rotate the rod slightly towards yourself and you will see a large gap between the horizontal cords. Take the right cord and weave under and over to the left to fill in this gap.
11 Both cords will now be on the left-hand side. Carefully slide the knot off the rod.
12 Insert your ball and tighten the knot. Manoeuvre the cord around the ball until you have an even shape.

MONKEY FIST

Using just one piece of cord, the Monkey Fist allows you to tie an attractive, neat ball knot.

1   Working from left to right, wrap the cord around your fingers three times.
2   Pass the right cord end behind the coils and up to the front, passing between your third and fourth fingers.
3   Make two more turns behind and up between your fingers, following the first one. Remove your fingers and pass the working cord through the middle of the knot.
4   Now pass the working end around and over the three horizontal coils, through the middle of the knot. Make two more turns following the first.
5   Now tighten every turn to make a regular ball shape.

CHAIN SINNET KNOT

Also known as the Chain Stitch or Monkey Chain, this knot is the macramé version of the crochet stitch. It forms an attractive, clean chain that can be used in multiple ways, from simple to complex.

1   Make a loop at the beginning of a long piece of cord.
2   Pass your fingers through this loop and grab hold of the longer end of the cord.
3   Pull this cord through until it makes another loop.
4   Keep repeating Steps 2 and 3.
5   When the chain is long enough, lock it by passing the working end of the cord through the final loop.

1

2

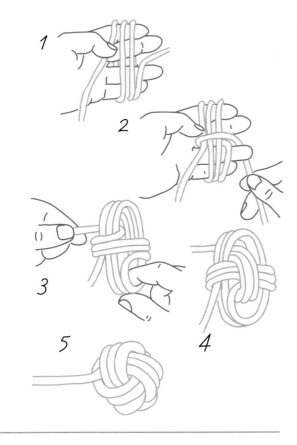

1

2

3

5

4

3

4

5

FISHTAIL KNOT

An easy-to-complete braid, the Fishtail is great for bracelets or straps. You will need two lengths of cord.

1 Using your first length of cord, double it over to create a loop. Make an Overhand knot (see page 115) at the end to secure the loop.

2 Take your second length of cord and begin a weaving pattern around the looped cord. First, take your working cord through the centre and over the right-hand cord, then repeat these moves:
   - Under the right hand cord
   - Over the left-hand cord
   - Under the left-hand cord
   - Over the right-hand cord.

1   2

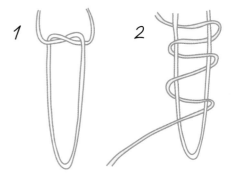

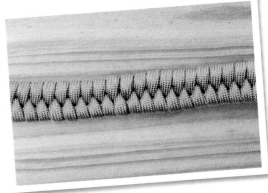

THREE- OR FOUR-STRAND BRAID KNOT

Once you master one braid pattern, it's very easy to master other braids. Let's get started with a traditional three- or four-strand braid.

THREE STRANDS

1   Line up your lengths. You can use Sellotape to hold them down at the beginning.
2   Start by taking the left-hand cord over the middle cord and under the right-hand cord.
3   Now repeat this pattern:
    - Left-hand cord over the middle cord.
    - Right-hand cord over the middle cord.

FOUR STRANDS

4   Line up your lengths. You can use Sellotape to hold them down.
5   Start by taking the cord two under cord three and over cord four.
6   Then take cord one over the new cord two.
7   Take the two centre cords and pass the left-hand cord over the right-hand cord.
8   Now repeat this pattern:
    - Outer left cord over second cord and into the middle.
    - Outer right cord under third cord and over the new second cord.

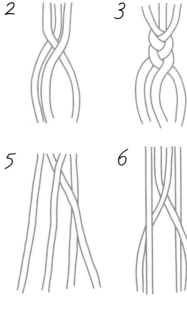

Three-Strand Braid (using double cords)

SIX-STRAND BRAID KNOT

This braid is similar in method to the Three- and Four-Strand Braid knot (see left), but we must use a slightly different pattern.

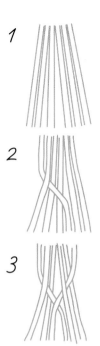

1 Line up all six lengths. You can use Sellotape to hold them down at the beginning.
2 To start, take the outer left cord under the second cord and over the third cord.
3 Now take the outer right cord over the fifth cord, under the fourth and over the new third cord.
4 Then repeat this pattern:
   • Left-hand cord under and over the middle cords from left to right.
   • Right-hand cord over, under and over the middle cords from right to left.

FOUR- OR EIGHT-STRAND DIAMOND BRAID KNOT

This braid can be completed with four or eight strands. To make an Eight-Strand Diamond Braid, simply double up each working strand. The technique is much the same as for a traditional Three- or Four-Strand Braid (see page 126), but we are aiming to achieve a rounder braid shape.

1 Split your cord into four working strands (if you have eight strands you should have four groups of two). You can use Sellotape to hold the cords down at the top.
2 To start, take the outer left cord over the second cord and under the third cord.
3 Take the outer right cord and pass it behind the two central cords.
4 Now take this same cord over and then under back to the right-hand side.
5 Take the outer left cord and pass it behind the two central cords.
6 Then take this same cord over and then under back to the left-hand side.
7 Repeat Steps 3-6 until you reach the desired length.

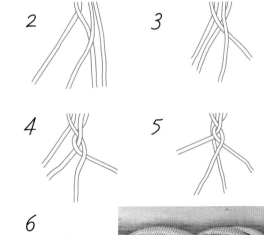

Eight-Strand Diamond Braid

Index